Get Your Sh*t Together
The Workbook

Created by:
Niecey Freeman

nieceyfreemanllc.com

Dedicated to:
My mentors: Gerald, Philecia, and Scott
The Mansfield Training Team (the homies)
My kids
My support system:
India, Erin, Angelique, Orlando, Tiffani, Edward
And most importantly, my grandfather (Papa)

CONTENTS

Get Ready

"I'm mega excited that you decided to start this journey with me! You've already taken the first step into getting your shit together - which was acknowledging that something needed to change - so let me congratulate you and welcome you to the exciting part... putting a plan together."

Is this program right for you?

- Are you ready to unleash your full potential?
- Feeling like you've lost your spark?
- Ready to reclaim your best self?
- Are you prepared to embrace your true calling?
- Ready to turn your dreams into reality?
- Are your goals feeling more like a mundane checklist?

If any of the above scenarios resonate with you, then this program is tailored to meet your needs. Embarking on this journey may not be without its challenges, as it requires a commitment to self-reflection and growth. Success demands honesty with oneself and the acknowledgment of personal responsibility. Regardless of external circumstances or perceived obstacles, the responsibility ultimately falls on you. It's a truth that may be uncomfortable to confront, yet essential for meaningful progress.

To get the best out of this program, don't skip ahead. There's not a magic fast forward button to achieve your goals. You have to put the work in.

Let's do this!

Create a space

- Carve out 1-2 hours during your most convenient days to dedicate solely to your goal-setting journey.
- Prioritize your mental well-being by ensuring you're in a positive headspace before diving in.
- Indulge in a brief 5-10 minute meditation session to center your mind and find clarity.
- Refresh your senses with a brisk walk or a soothing yoga session to invigorate your creativity.
- Encourage yourself with a motivational mantra, like "It's time to get my shit together," to fuel your determination.
- Minimize interruptions by silencing your phone and creating a distraction-free environment.
- Enhance your focus with calming background music to elevate your productivity.
- Know when to take breaks; when the creativity wanes, put the pen down and return to it later with renewed energy.

80% of New Year Resolutions fail

Also, when it comes to achieving goals, there's currently an 8% success rate*. So there's plenty of room for us to win!

*from www.inc.com

Does it work?

Getting your shit together is a process, an experience, and a milestone. It allows you to form positive habits, improve the quality of your life, and celebrate success. Things may happen that will cause you to shift focus. When that happens, come back to this workbook and make the necessary changes.

The GYST program is divided into 4 categories:

Financial
- How much money do you want/need to make and why?

Personal
- How are you going to take care of you?

Family
- What are you going to do to build better relationships with your family?

Professional
- Where do you want to be in your career?

While you are working on your goal setting, it is important not to combine categories. For example, your professional goals should not include where you want to be financially.

Based on your previous experience with setting goals, you may choose to get started immediately and complete the workbook in one sitting or you may want to divide it into chunks. If you are a "start/stopper" like me, smaller portions work best. I don't want you to just fill out the form. I want you to actually succeed, so take as much time as you need. I will say this- if you divvy it up you will have several different checkpoints which may complicate things a bit.

Does this program actually work?

Heck yeah it does!

Back in 2014, I got serious about setting goals, with help from my first mentor, Gerald. My first financial goal was pretty straightforward: I wanted to earn as much money annually as my age. At 30, I was bringing in $27,000 a year, which was the most I'd ever made up to that point. Looking ahead, I aimed to hit $35,000 by the time I hit 35. Some folks might think, "Is that all?" But hey, for me, it was a big step up.

Using the format in this workbook, I have been able to achieve more success than I ever thought possible. I met my financial goal within two years and I make a lot more than $35,000/year now with not only my business and with a full-time job, but other streams of revenue as well. All according to plan.

Now it's your turn.

How is this different?

Simple, you have me now. My contact information will be listed in this workbook and I am here to help guide you every step of the way. I haven't released this to the world yet, so I don't know how many text or emails I'll receive. So for now, let's say it may take up to 24-48 hours for a response. I want you to reach out to me any time you:

- need a push
- want to share your success
- are frustrated and need guidance

I got you!

I know exactly what it's like to be in a dark place with no idea what direction to turn. If I could, I would make sure no one else feels like that...ever. I love hearing the excitement of a client who achieved a goal they never thought possible. This is my purpose and there's no better feeling. I get goosebumps just thinking about it.

The GYST program has 5 segments. In this workbook, we will cover two; define your why, and set realistic goals

Define Your Why

Your why is your purpose. It sets you apart from everyone else. It's your motivating force.

Set Realistic Goals

Realistic goals are your golden ticket to the life you've only previously seen in dreams.

Define your Why

Repeat after me:

"My why is mine, not my kids', my spouse's, parents', or anyone else's. It...is...MINE!"

Some parents can't get out of caregiver mode long enough to focus on themselves. Way too many people say, "my kids are my why."

NO, your kids are your responsibility. There's this unspoken parental guilt that forces us, as parents, to say we live for our kids. You do everything you can for them until they are off to the workforce or college and by the time you're able to live your best life, your old ass is tired. Live your best life NOW!

Your why should not include anyone but YOU. Think of it this way- taking care of yourself enables you to be a better parent, a better husband/wife/partner, and a better example to those closest to you.

Got it? OK. Let's do some activities!

●●●●●

It's time to put YOU first

●●●●●

A Letter to Yourself

Use the space below to write a letter to motivate yourself. Come back to it whenever you need that extra push.

Instructions:

1. Decide how far in the future you want to ready your letter and set a calendar reminder
2. Talk about what's going on in your life currently
3. Talk about your hopes and aspirations
4. Ask yourself questions
5. Express gratitude and kindness to yourself

Great! Now circle the one that means the absolute most to you
with zero parental guilt.

What you circled is now or already was your why. It's your motivating force. It's why you roll yourself out of bed in the morning (other than having to pee). Take a moment to soak it all in.

Alright, so who are your top 5 people? They all need to be people you know, that are close to you, and the ones you spend the most time with. FYI, your kids don't go here either. Also, please refrain from numbering them.

My Top 5:

Now, since you can't do awesome shit with basic people, you may need to make a few changes. If someone in your top 5 is toxic- and don't kid yourself, you know what toxic traits look like- they have got to go! If someone is very close to you and is not on this list, give them less energy or cut them out completely. Make this happen as soon as possible. Here, I even have suggested scripting for you:

"My apologies for being so out of touch, I'm getting my shit together."

Keep in mind that some people will take it personal, but also keep in mind that you are not obligated to explain yourself.

Roadblocks

You can maneuver around some of your roadblocks, but there are some that claim a permanent residence in you mind and can prevent you from believing in yourself such as childhood trauma and abusive relationships. Another hard truth is, life isn't going to hold back on you, so don't you fucking dare hold back on yourself. If you find yourself stuck remember why you're doing this in the first place. This is YOUR life. If you fall back, brush yourself off and start over. You have to keep going, You have to remove the toxicity from your life. You have to live!

Common Roadblocks

- Waiting for someone else to step in and save the day. *Unless you're a cartoon princess, it's probably not going to work out that way*
- Traditions. *You don't have to do what anyone else does*
- Waiting on your significant other to "act right" so you can focus.
- You think you're not good enough to be successful
- Conditioning. *I don't know if you knew this, but you don't have to do what anyone else does*
- You're convinced that it's not the right time or you don't have enough time.
- Fear of failure

Listen, your brain is your biggest hype man. If you think "I can't do this", your brain is going to say *"you're absolutely right", We suck*! BUT if you tell your brain "I got this", your brain is going to respond *"Heck yeah! Let's go!"*

● ● ● ● ●

Life isn't going to hold back on you, so don't you dare hold back on yourself.

● ● ● ● ●

Let's discuss what's holding you back. Roadblocks present themselves at every single step of the way. We will not only list them, we will also figure out how to swerve around them.

My Roadblocks

Circle 3 of your roadblocks

In the box below, list things that you think could help you with the roadblocks you selected. A good example would be "to learn more about (insert roadblock)". Another example would be "talk to a personal consultant". If this is a response you have, you're in luck, I happen to know one. List as many resources as possible.

What/who could help?

Goal Setting

You may have heard of different types of goal setting plans represented with acronyms and such. For some, those methods help. However, with a success rate of only 8 percent, I think it's safe to say that these methods are not as effective as we would like to believe. The thing about setting these types of goals is that you're on your own, mostly. No one is with you to give you that push. You're missing a critical piece and that's accountability.

During the course of your goal setting, I am here for you. I'm only an email or a text message away.

I only have two requirements for the goal setting you will do with me, everything else is built in. The requirements are to **BE REALISTIC** and **CHALLENGE YOURSELF**.

I can't tell you how many clients I've seen say they will be a millionaire by next year with zero effort. Is it possible, yes, anything is possible. It's the probability that varies. I have detailed instructions laid out for each category. If your goal is to make substantially more, you will need to chart your path to how you're going to get there.

Alright, let's set some goals! I have listed an example of a goal I set for myself in 2019. The secret is to start at 3 years and work yourself down to what you will need to do daily. So, if your plan is to become a public speaker in 3 years, every checkpoint will have a goal that you'll need to achieve. Remember, this could make your brain hurt so take your time.

The example I have below breaks down every module.

Types of goals

This category will represent different types of goals including:

Financial -How much money do you want/need to make and why
Personal -How are you going to take care of you?
Family -What are you going to do to build better relationships with your family?
Professional -Where do you want to be in your career?

Friendly reminder, please do not mix categories. The only goal that should have a target for income is financial just like the only goal that includes your family should be the family category, and so on.

There are 8 Checkpoints

- 3 Years
- 2 Years
- 1 Year
- 9 Months
- 6 Months
- 3 Months
- Monthly
- Daily

Each checkpoint gives you an opportunity to monitor your progress and readjust as needed. Each date should be the appropriate time frame from your "today's" date.

Example (from my actual goal setting)

Professional

Today: December 15, 2019

Date

3 Years

I will be a key note speaker with 3 publishings under my belt

Dec 15, 2022

2 Years

Attain a key note speaker as a mentor. Host webinars and small conferences

Dec 15, 2021

1 Year

2nd publishing / release Merch

Dec 15, 2020

9 Months

Assist and support other small business including pro bono work

Sept 15, 2020

6 Months

Attend 2 Networking Events per quarter

June 15, 2020

3 Months

Launch Business and Website

March 15, 2020

Weekly

Read 1-3 hours (development material) Asses and readjust

Thursday Check in. 2pm

Daily

Create and complete a daily task list Positivity checks throughout the day

7pm check in

Intentionally left blank

Best Practices

- Only 1-2 goals per checkpoint
- Be sure to set dates and/or times for check-ins (for weekly and daily). This will keep you on track.
- If you can't think of anything, put your pen down and or walk away for a moment.
- After every checkpoint, save the date to your calendar.
    - For example say, "Hey Siri, set a reminder to assess and re-adjust every Thursday at 5pm."
- Send me a text when you hit a checkpoint and let me know if you accomplished your goal or if you need help re-adjusting.

Let Siri, Alexa, or Google Assistant do the work for you!

Type of Goal

Today:

3 Years

What is your ultimate goal?

2 Years

What do you need to have accomplished in two years achieve your 3-year goal?

1 Year

What do you need to have accomplished in one year to achieve your 2-year goal?

9 Months

What do you need to have accomplished in 9 months to achieve your 1 year goal?

6 Months

What do you need to have accomplished in 6 months to achieve your 9 month goal?

3 Months

What do you need to have accomplished in 3 months to achieve your 6-month goal?

Weekly

What do you need to do once a week in order to achieve your goal?

Daily

What do you need to do every day in order to achieve your goal?

Date

What will be the date exactly 3 years from today?

What will be the date exactly 2 years from today?

What will be the date exactly 1 year from today?

What will be the date exactly 9 months from today?

What will be the date exactly 6 months from today?

What will be the date exactly 3 months from today?

What day of the week are you going to monitor your progress?

What time will you monitor your progress?

Financial

Today:

3 Years

Date

2 Years

1 Year

9 Months

6 Months

3 Months

Weekly

Daily

Personal

Today: ________________________

3 Years

Date

2 Years

1 Year

9 Months

6 Months

3 Months

Weekly

Daily

Family

Today: _______________

3 Years

2 Years

1 Year

9 Months

6 Months

3 Months

Weekly

Daily

Date

Intentionally left blank

Professional

Today:

3 Years

Date

2 Years

1 Year

9 Months

6 Months

3 Months

Weekly

Daily

Intentionally left blank

Daily Tracker

We're going to start by tracking your daily goals for 3 months.

Tracking your daily goals is an effective way to start forming positive habits. Here are some tips:

- Start small
  - Begin with task that are so simple, it's hard not to continue
- Break larger task into small bits
  - If one of your daily task is to work out more, start with 10-15 minute workouts and work your way up
- Schedule time
  - Set reminders to complete task as a particular time every day
- If you fall, get your ass up and keep going
  - Missed a day, how about a week? Don't beat yourself up. Success comes to those who don't give up.

Write down the daily goals you set for yourself here:

Financial

Personal

Professional

Family

Success comes to those who don't give up

Intentionally left blank

Daily Tracker

Mark for each day you were able to achieve your daily habits. This tracks 45 days broken down by 5 days each. Challenge yourself not to 45 days, but 5 days at a time. I believe in you! I also have daily tracker magnets available on my website. You can also cut out this page and stick it to your fridge.

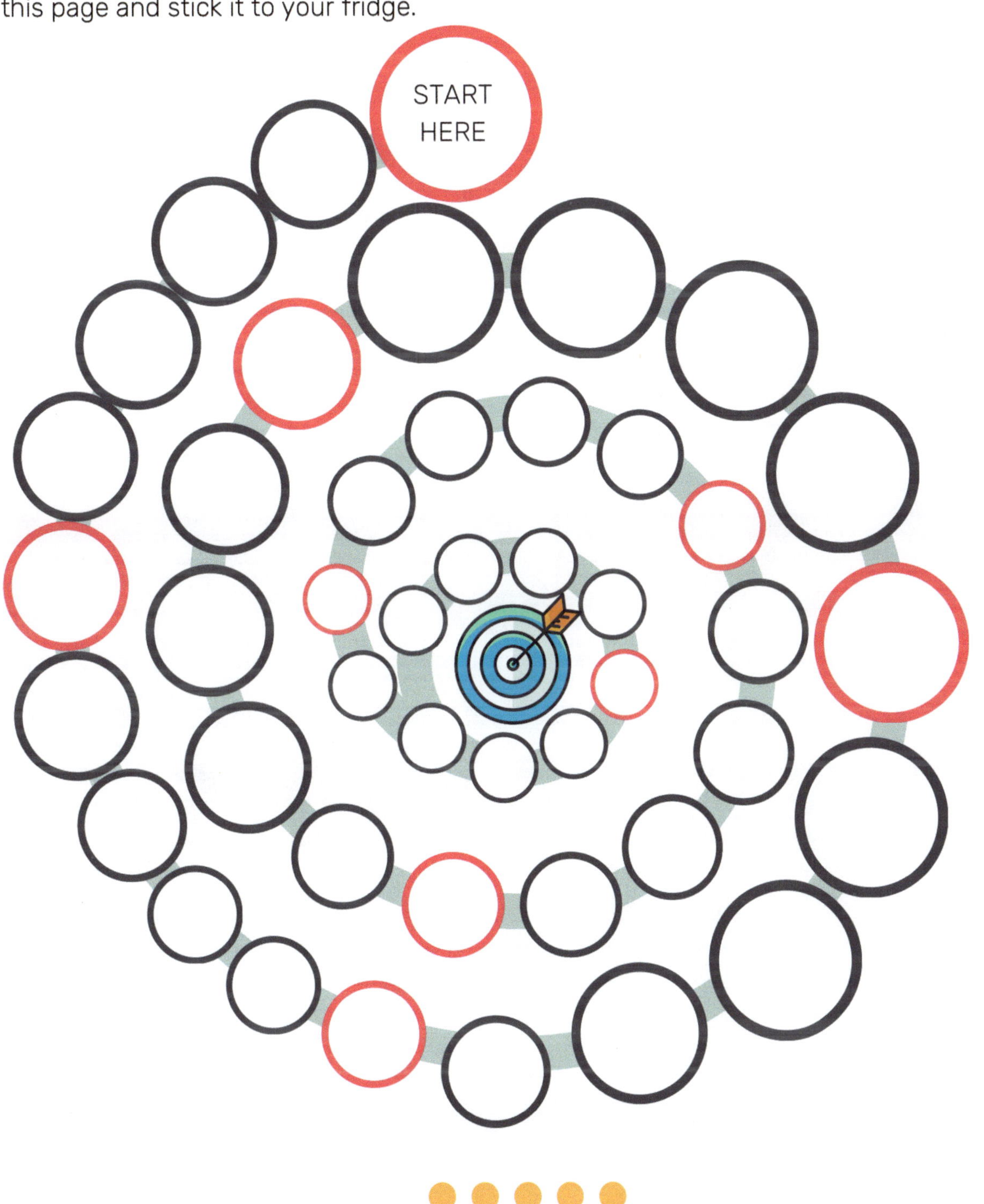

Daily Tracker

YAAAAAAS!!

Now that you have 45 days complete, let's do another 45. You got this!

Reminders and Next Steps

- Create calendar reminders for checkpoints
- Step away when you get stuck and take a brain break
  - Schedule a session or text me if you need help
- Be sure your checkpoints are milestones that you need to hit in order to achieve your 3-year goal
- Make sure you have 1-2 milestones per checkpoint
- Challenge yourself
- Don't forget to have fun and celebrate your success

Congratulations on completing your Goal Setting!
-Go Celebrate-

About Me

I'm from Martinsville, a small town in southern Virginia, located in the foothills of the Blue Ridge Mountains. I was mostly raised by my grandparents. I moved in with my mother when I started high school. Throughout my teenage years, I was constantly in trouble at school for fighting -and sometimes with the law.

I joined the Army when I was 18 because I wanted to have a better life and because I was determined to get a canary yellow Mustang GT convertible. I settled for a black one and it was not a convertible. It was my first real goal. I served in the Army for 6 years. It was an adventure, but I made lots of bad choices. Life didn't get any easier as a civilian.

Rock Bottom

In 2012, I found myself as a single mom, juggling the responsibilities of raising three young children. Relocating from Martinsville to Shelby, Ohio, I entered a challenging chapter where I earned a modest wage of $9.25 per hour. Unfortunately, the living conditions in Shelby proved to be less than ideal, compounded by the presence of a neighbor grappling with a severe drug addiction. The unsettling discovery of needles scattered in our yard on multiple occasions only added to the already difficult circumstances.

One fateful day, my refrigerator decided to call it quits. When I reached out to my landlord, they informed me that it would take a grueling three days to replace it. With my food stamps already depleted and my pockets empty, I faced the grim reality of tossing away all the groceries I had purchased as they spoiled within just two days. Left with no other options, I divided a single can of corn among myself and my three children for dinner. The crushing disappointment of this moment served as a wake-up call, igniting a fierce determination within me to turn my life around once and for all.

The Vision

Determined never to endure such hardships again, I took charge of my destiny. I went to work the next day and expressed my readiness for advancement, and dedicated myself to this goal. My diligence paid off as I secured a promotion within months. With guidance from my mentor, Gerald, I crafted a strategic 5-year plan. Through relentless effort, I achieved promotions every 2-3 years and surpassed my financial aspirations.

I attended a vision board workshop facilitated by another mentor, Philecia, in January of 2019. Watching her made me realize that I was putting my passion in the wrong places. I wanted to do what she was doing because I knew I would be awesome at it too. I wanted to help people who were like me in 2012... all the potential in the world and little to no direction. I started my LLC, and now I am living my purpose.

Intentionally left blank

Contact me

🌐 www.nieceyfreemanllc.com

✉️ nfreeman@nieceyfreemanllc.com

💬 Text me: 513.568.6676

I also...

- Conduct 1x1 Goal Setting sessions (1-2 hours)
- Coaching (1 hour sessions)
- Sell Merch
- Do Resume Makeovers
- GYST Book **COMING SOON!**

Intentionally left blank

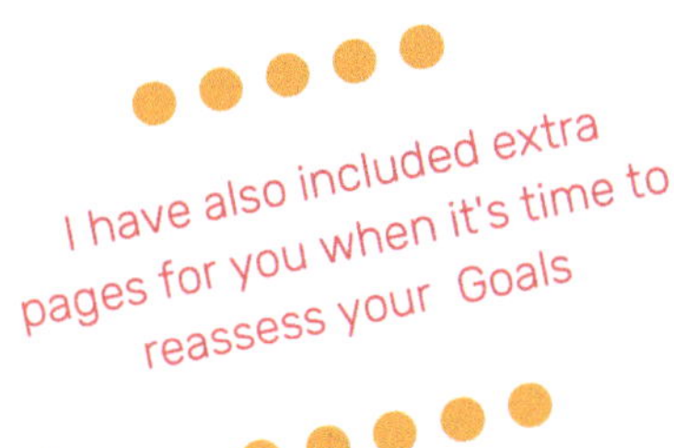

Bonus Pages

Today:

3 Years

Date

2 Years

1 Year

9 Months

6 Months

3 Months

Weekly

Daily

Financial

Today:

3 Years

Date

2 Years

1 Year

9 Months

6 Months

3 Months

Weekly

Daily

Personal

Today: _______________

3 Years

Date

2 Years

1 Year

9 Months

6 Months

3 Months

Weekly

Daily

Family

Today:

3 Years

Date

2 Years

1 Year

9 Months

6 Months

3 Months

Weekly

Daily

Professional

Today:

3 Years

Date

2 Years

1 Year

9 Months

6 Months

3 Months

Weekly

Daily

Daily Tracker

Bonus Tracker

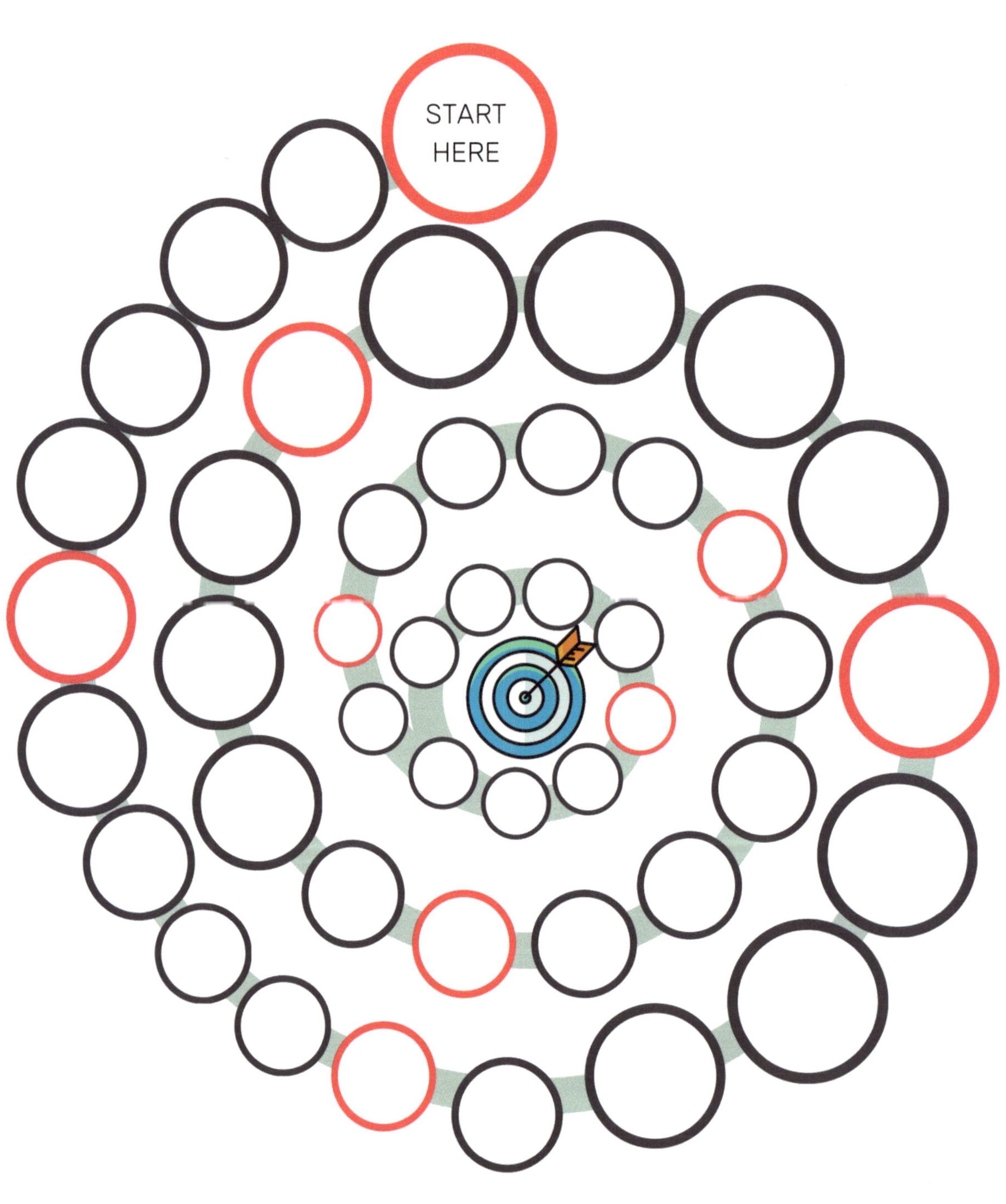

Intentionally left blank

Daily Tracker

Bonus Tracker

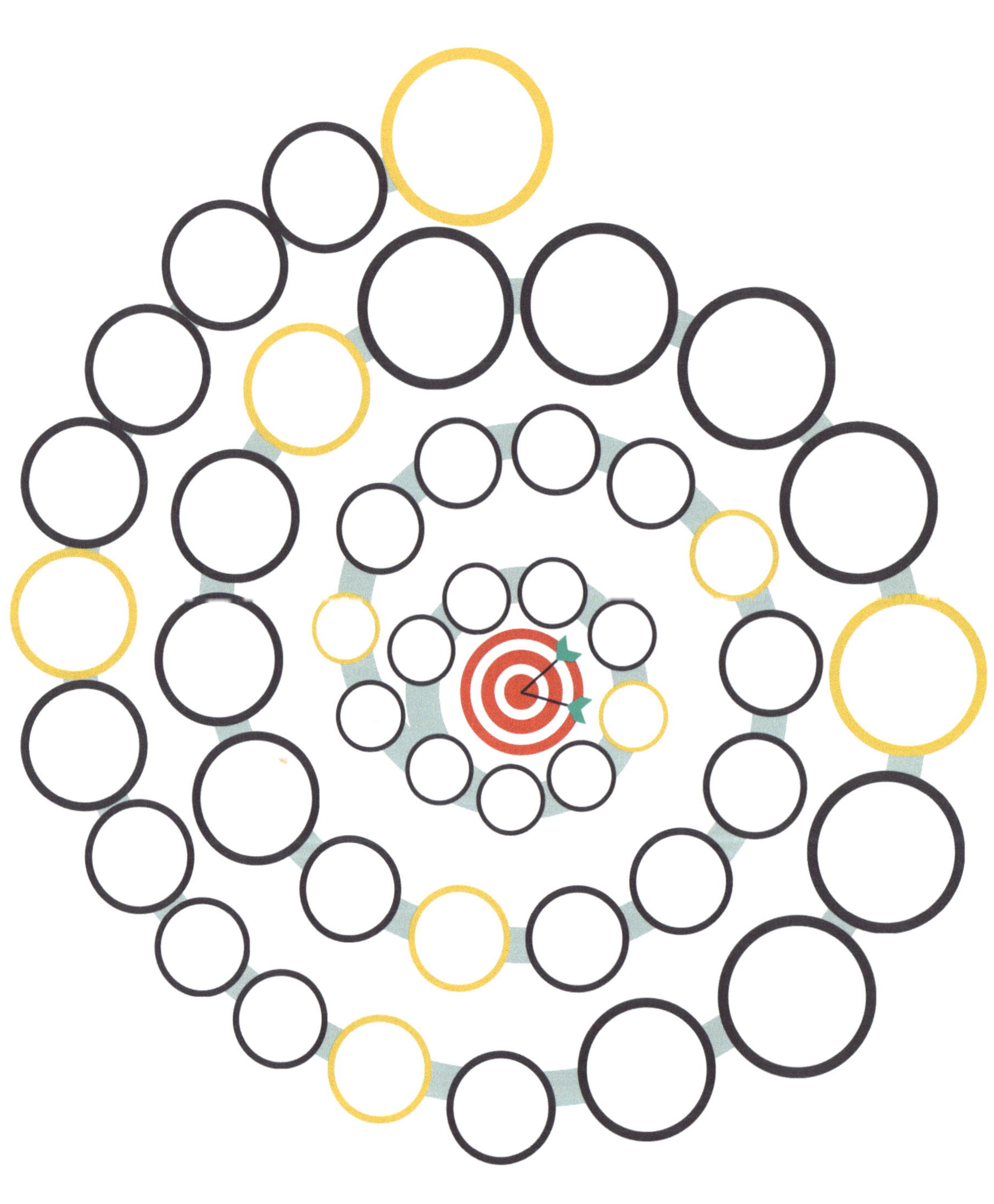

Financial

Today: ______________________

| **3 Years** | **Date** |

| **2 Years** | |

| **1 Year** | |

| **9 Months** | |

| **6 Months** | |

| **3 Months** | |

| **Weekly** | |

| **Daily** | |

Personal

Today:

3 Years

Date

2 Years

1 Year

9 Months

6 Months

3 Months

Weekly

Daily

Family

Today:

3 Years

Date

2 Years

1 Year

9 Months

6 Months

3 Months

Weekly

Daily

Professional

Today:

Date

3 Years

2 Years

1 Year

9 Months

6 Months

3 Months

Weekly

Daily

Daily Tracker

Bonus Tracker

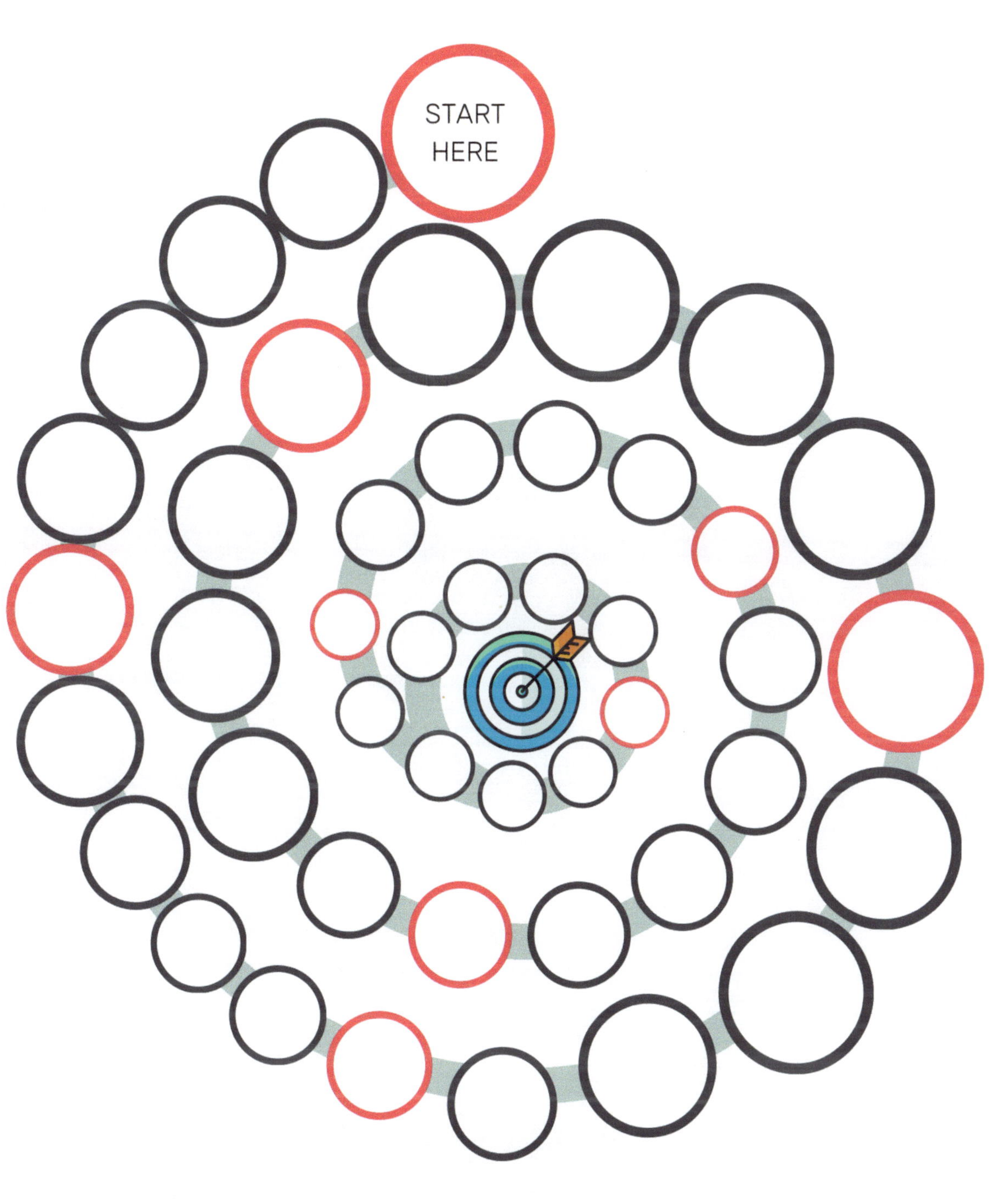

Intentionally left blank

Daily Tracker

Bonus Tracker

Intentionally left blank

Thank you for allowing me to assist you with getting your shit together! If ever you need help, I will be happy to assist. This program is highly effective as long as you stick to it. Please don't be afraid to share your success or opportunities with me.

I wish you the best. Hope to hear from you soon!

Love,

Get Your Sh*t Together
The Workbook

nieceyfreemanllc.com